The Inspirational Autobiography of
SIEON C. ROBERTS, SR.

Panting After *His* Presence

When Striving after God becomes a Lifestyle

Thigpen **W**riters **G**roup
Publishing Perfection

Panting After His Presence

Sieon C. Roberts, Sr.

© **Copyright 2006**
Thigpen Writers Group

All rights reserved. No portion of this book may be reproduced, scanned, stored in a retrieval system, transmitted in any form or by any means - electronic, mechanical, photocopy, recording, or any other - except for brief quotations in printed reviews without written permission of the publisher. Please do not participate in or encourage piracy of copyrighted materials in violation of the author's rights. Purchase only authorized editions.

Library of Congress Cataloging-in-Publication Data

Sieon C. Roberts, Sr.
Panting After His Presence

ISBN: 0-9777697-2-0
1. Christians – Religious Life.
Printed in the United States of America

Thigpen Writers Group
Anthony KaDarrell Thigpen, Editor in Chief
Copy, Cover Design, and Layout Editor

Content

Acknowledgements	pages xi-xii

Preface
Lobdell's Legacy Lives in Me   13-18
By Dr. Cato Brooks

Foreword
Anointing Produced in the Press   19-24
By Brandon Jacobs

Introduction   25-30
Gathering the Broken Pieces

Chapter I   31-38
Covenant of Bondage
Her Marriage; My Abuse

Chapter II   39-48
Way of Escape
Running From Misery

Chapter III   49-56
Land of Promise
Destination Determines Destiny

Chapter IV	57-64
Forsaken	
The Man In The Mirror	
Chapter V	65-78
Searching for Identity	
Manmade Mistakes, God Made Miracles	
Chapter VI	79-88
Torn into a Million Pieces	
Consequences Of Covenant Breaking	
Chapter VII	89-100
Humility, Honor, and Hope	
Let The Meek Rejoice	
Chapter VIII	101-106
The Power of Forgiveness	
Faith Without Forgiveness Fails	
Chapter IX	107-115
Legacy of Leadership	
I Am Born To Preach The Gospel	

-x-

Acknowledgements

I give praises to my Lord and Savior for adding value to my once worthless life. I now understand that my trials and challenges are designed to produce supernatural power. This book is a tribute to the faithfulness of the Father.

Anita, the love of my life, thank you for listening, understanding, and praying. With you, I've learned what it truly means to be one with your spouse. Our matrimony is the pinnacle of my life.

Giara, Carl, Sieon, Jr. and Jeremiah - my beautiful daughter and three sons. I promise to be for you, what no man has been for me, a father. Together, the four of you bring me exceedingly great joy.

Delpha (Momma), and my two sisters Arke'ya (Beautiful Flower) and Hawah (Eve), from the depths of my heart I thank you for always standing by my side. Your continued support is immeasurable, and my life is a mural of the love we share.

New Hope M.B. Church, my spiritual family, after

57-years of faithfulness in inner-city ministry, you are my greatest inspiration. You make up a congregation of believers that endures the worse, but our sufferings are not worthy to be compared to the glory God reveals in us. New Hope is where new hope begins.

Baptist Ministers Conference of Gary and Vicinity, your northwest Indiana presence is invaluable. As pastors, your leadership, involvement, and unity are foundational pillars for the people of our community. Thank you for acknowledging my youth, accepting my input, and lending me wisdom. Your guidance is valued and appreciated.

Anthony KaDarrell Thigpen, my editor, thank you for carefully developing my thoughts and causing this book to become a reality. Also, thank you for sharing your God-given gifts of writing and revelation. Lastly, I value our friendship, and appreciate you for extending yourself beyond measure.

Lobdell's Legacy Lives in Me

PREFACE

By Dr. Cato Brooks

Preface by Dr. Cato Brooks

Lobdell's Legacy Lives In Me

Preface

In reading this book you will be touched by the sincerity of the author, Sieon Roberts, Sr. It is so pleasant, gratifying, and reassuring to see how the Spirit of God continues blessing him on so many different levels. His testimony is one of triumph!

With great forethought, he bears his innermost thoughts. Roberts has journeyed from the life of a troubled teen and struggling young adult to a 26-year-old senior pastor, who has overcome countless adversities. *Panting After His Presence* reaches into the hearts of readers, captivating them with his victorious testimony.

Roberts has experienced difficulties ranging from low self-esteem, street violence, attempted suicide, a failed marriage, to unfruitful relationships. However, through the grace of God, he defied all odds, persevered and used his obstacles as stepping-stones to stand, depend, trust, and lean on God. When a deer races along the streams of water brooks, they feed off green pastures, and use drinking water

Preface by Dr. Cato Brooks

to hide their scent from the enemy. Just as the deer pants after water brooks, Roberts is chasing after God's presence. Go with him and discover the makings of an anointed man of faith.

This autobiography unveils his life story in a truthful, powerful, and encouraging manner. I'm confident that this book will inspire you, as much, if not more, than it does myself. Roberts testimony is an exemplary example that enables readers to rest assure that *all things are possible through Christ who strengthens us*.

While reading this book, you will be brilliantly enthused by thought-provoking words of wisdom and the strength. My prayer is that believers and non-believers alike, of all ages, will read this book and take the message to heart. Perhaps your life, and that of your loved ones, will benefit from this never-before-told testimony.

God will use the pieces of your broken vessel and make *you* whole. Sieon Roberts, Sr. is my nephew. This book explains how we are connected biologically and spiritually. I am proud that he follows in the legacy of the ministry of Christ.

Lobdell's Legacy Lives In Me

Through his bravery, candor, inspiration, love, and sincerity, his life is a display of God's ever-working-power in today's generation.

Dr. Cato Brooks, Jr. attended Southern University in Baton Rouge, Louisiana, however, he continued his studies at the University of Kansas, Bachelor of Science sociology program. He later attended the Mid-America Baptist Seminary at Ouachita Baptist University where he earned his Bachelors and Masters. At Indiana Christian University he earned his Doctorate of Divinity. Dr. Brooks is founder and senior pastor of Tree of Life M.B. Church in Gary, Indiana. September 2003, he published *Studies in Ephesians*. Pastor Brooks is formerly Chaplain for the Gary Police Department and Moderator for the Northern Indiana Missionary Baptist District Association.

Anointing Produced In The Press

FOREWORD

By Brandon Jacobs

Foreword by Brandon Jacobs

Anointing Produced In The Press

Pastor Sieon Roberts, Sr. is a humble man of God with a powerful anointing. Roberts had to experience countless challenges, sorrow, and pain to gain godly promotion. His life puts people in mind of a modern day David, King of Israel. David possessed a noteworthy relationship with God, although he made many mistakes. David's mistakes include peeping on Bathsheba's nakedness, and then impregnating her during an adulterous affair. Afterward, he sent her husband to war to die, and underestimated God's ability by numbering his soldiers.

As a child, beaten and abused, Sieon Chontel never imagined serving in the pastorate one of the most prominent churches in Gary, Indiana. Much like David, who Samuel anointed king while he was still a child herding sheep, God also anointed Sieon while he was seemingly under-qualified. God's eyes saw the king inside both kids. While reading this autobiography you will go beneath the surface of Roberts struggles, and then discover that God produces anointing under great pressure.

Most people selfishly want God to anoint them with supernatural power so that they can "look good," so to speak, amongst other preachers and

Foreword by Brandon Jacobs

church-goers. Anointing is not for showmanship. It's acquired by those who persevere through life's most difficult challenges and circumstance.

Consider how King Saul chased after David to kill him. For those who are familiar with the story, imagine David's anguished, frustration, disappointment, discontentment, and sorrow. But Saul's acts of hatred caused David to mature, and strengthened his foundation of faith in God. David maintained a pure approach and a positive attitude throughout the situation. A pure, pleasant, and mature foundation amid challenges is what produces a supernatural anointing in the life of believers. The oil that Samuel poured on David as a child represents the anointing that God produced in his life. Every believer has to endure some difficult experiences in order operate under God's anointing.

With this understanding of how anointing is produced, we're able to understand why Elisha asked for a "hard thing" when he requested a double portion of the prophet Elijah's anointing (II Kings 2:9). A double portion of anointing is to say, "I'm willing to endure double the trouble." That's exactly what 26-year-old Roberts has done, he's triumphed

Anointing Produced In The Press

over troublesome and shameful circumstances, and God has given him double anointing. "For your shame ye shall have double; and for confusion they shall rejoice in their portion..." (Isaiah 61:7).

Panting After His Presence is such an extraordinary book because it tells the untold story of how Roberts has been broken, squeezed, and pressed with trial and tribulations. The anointing oil spoken of in the Bible is produced when olives are properly pressed until its liquid completely secrete. We are like those olives, and when we go through the worse mess, life's most difficult challenges, and our least desirable trials, God is producing supernatural power in us. Roberts has made his life an open book so that believers and non-believers alike can experience the glory of God. Upon reading this book readers will walk away with a new perspective, because this untold story is riveting. Let's chase after God's presence, and experience his anointing.

Introduction

Gathering The Broken Pieces

Panting After His Presence/Introduction

God brings us through life's most difficult challenges, and he gives us testimonies to remind us of his goodness.

Memories of my childhood are vague and distorted, but the Holy Spirit is helping me piece the puzzle of my life together. Without the knowledge of who God is, I could never effectively discover the truth of who I am, and who I'm destined to become. Today, because I've been introduced to God's grace, my life has logic, and my vision is clear.

The first three Bible verses introduces the triune nature of God - he is Father of creation, Son of man, and Holy Spirit of promise. The first chapter of Genesis also says we are made in God's image and likeness. As a result, we are body, soul, and spirit. Our true identity is scripted into the written word of God. Our individual destiny is buried deep within his mysteries, and God is waiting to resurrect us. The Bible does not only enable us to understand the nature of God, it also illuminates our purpose for existing.

Gathering The Broken Pieces

The more we study God's word and define ourselves according to scripture, the sculpture of our identity becomes an empowered reality.

> **Instead, of transforming into God's likeness, far too many self-righteous individuals misinterpret scriptures trying to justify their imperfections.**

Instead, of transforming into God's likeness, far too many self-righteous individuals misinterpret scriptures trying to justify their imperfections. We are nothing without God, although it's difficult for mainstream society to embrace this reality. God never fails, and he always serves an integral part in our lives, even before birth.

I've experienced heart wrenching disappointments, including abuse, depression, defeat, and divorce. I've been overlooked, stepped on, misused, ignored, belittled, lied on, and manipulated. But the relationship I share with God makes every difficult experience meaningful and worthwhile.

When I apply God's word to my past and

Panting After His Presence/Introduction

present circumstances, every void, heartache, and disappointment disappears. I understand that my praise and my worship are valuable, my life is meaningful, and it is because of God that I exist.

In many ways my life has mirrored the life of Moses, because family and friends have journeyed with me from the pit to the promise land. On countless occasions I've messed up. I've even wanted to quit, and had every reason to do so, but I didn't. God honors those who persevere. When life seemed senseless, I grew frustrated and almost fainted. Now, it's clear to me that God requires us to share in His suffering, so that we can experience his glory.

This book is a collection of inspirational memoirs. A true triumphant testimony to help others gather the broken pieces and experience God's promises.

Just like a deer racing along the streams of water brooks, so does my soul chase after God's presence. As a young pastor, perhaps some people think I've achieved my greatest height too soon, but not so. I refuse to forfeit any promise God has for me, and neither should you.

Gathering The Broken Pieces

Pursue God like never before. Discover your purpose, and find the missing pieces needed to put life in perspective. Regardless of status quo, bank accounts, age, or education, God has a specific plan for everybody. Social success without an intimate relationship with Christ is ultimate failure. God wants our total submission. He desires our undivided attention. In his presence we have peace, protection, power, and promises. This is why we must race in pursuit of his presence, and let nothing hinder our stride. Let the chase begin.

Panting After His Presence/Introduction

Chapter I
Covenant into Bondage

Her Marriage; My Abuse

Covenant into Bondage/ Chapter 1

God manifested a miracle at Methodist Hospital Northlake in Gary, Indiana.

October 7, 1979, Delpha Roberts gave birth to me, Sieon Chontel Roberts, Sr. Carnal-minded naysayers claim that nothing good comes from Gary, but that's not true. Contrary to the report of the-late Peter Jennings, 60-Minutes news reporter, the people of Gary are not forsaken.

Here's how it all started. During the 1980's, Indianapolis was largely populated with African exchange students. Indiana University Purdue University Indianapolis (IUPUI) is where Liberian student Lucia Taylor-Fahnbullah and Delpha Vonita Lobdell became best friends. In fact, the two women developed a vibrant sister-to-sister relationship. They shared similarities, and in many ways, they bridged the gap between the African and African-American cultures. Lucia taught Delpha how to prepare exotic and domestic African dishes. Delpha returned the gesture by teaching Lucia how to cook southern soul

Her Marriage; My Abuse

food.

They both had time to spare. Lucia temporarily left her husband and newborn daughter in Liberia West Africa to study nursing in America. The year was 1981, and Delpha's one-year-old son remained about 154 highway miles away. I lived in Gary with my grandparents, Clarence and Lesserean Lobdell. In absence of those they loved, the two women shared life as sisters.

According to the Baptist Ministry Conference of Gary and Vicinity, the-late Reverend Clarence Lobdell, is one of Gary's most remembered pastors. He served at New Hope Missionary Baptist Church for 35-years. He believed that the church is the apple of God's eye. In addition, he called me his pride and joy. At age two, toddling in the shadows of my grandfather's path, everyday I spent time learning to imitate men of God, namely the Baptist ministers of northwest Indiana.

Meanwhile, Lucia, with her joyous and outgoing personality, introduced Mom to one of her Liberian counterparts. His name is Armah Roberts. The surname Roberts is not of African origin. After

Covenant into Bondage/ Chapter 1

the emancipation of slavery, many Africans managed to return to Liberia. They used the last-names of former slave masters. In case you didn't know, during slavery, languages, names, and cultural identities are stolen. Therefore, Armah represents a small percentage of native Africans with American originated names. Much like the affects of slavery, Armah changed my life forever.

The nightmare started the evening of Halloween 1981. Armah escorted Mom on a blind date to dinner and a movie. She had no idea what the future had in store for her. People should be careful when seeking a spouse. The comedy, *Arthur*, sparked a needed sense of humor during their boring date. Mom says she glared into Armah's eyes with respect, but no romance, no connection, and no sense of passion. Instead, she sat in discontentment harboring thoughts about an old fling.

Mom's listening ear is apparently what Armah needed. Five days after their first date, he purchased her some $52 Calvin Klein jeans from Blocks Department Store. She was impressed by his flattering gesture. Suddenly, thoughts about her old boyfriend dissolved, and her new relationship began

Her Marriage; My Abuse

to take on a new form.

According to Mom, Armah is handsome, but he's always been hideous to me. I suppose I was too young to recall the days of his alleged good looks. Armah is 5-feet 7-inches, and weighs about 145 pounds. His miniature afro is always kinked into small unmanageable knots. His facial features are extremely animated; slanted eyes, pitched-dark-skin, tiny ears, and big-pink-lips. Well, they say beauty is in the eye of the beholder. Obviously Mom saw something that others didn't. The man looked horrible. I will say, he has a great personality. He's humorous, quick-witted, and sometimes even thoughtful. The more he hung around, Armah's personality grew on Mom.

March 1982, five months after their first date, Armah asked her to marry him. Mom deserved better, but she compromised. Armah bought her nice things and made her smile, as a result, she said yes. Seven months after their first date, May 1982 they wed in Gary.

Over the next few years, things changed. A new marriage, with new responsibilities, including a

Covenant into Bondage/ Chapter 1

two-year-old son, resulted in Armah's decision to drop out of college to work longer hours. For two-years, we attended Unity Fellowship Baptist Church in Indianapolis. Although Mom hadn't dedicated her life to God, as a pastor's daughter she understood the importance of church attendance. By this time, she was pregnant with Hawah, her name means Eve. Naming children is important to Armah's African heritage. Initially, he wanted to name my sister Benuh. Mom adamantly refused! Hawah was born February 28, 1984.

I toddled around poorly enunciating Bible verses until age four. That's when the Roberts family relocated to Norfolk, Virginia. We moved because Armah found stable employment with the United States Navy.

While living in Norfolk, Mom attended an at-home Bible study where she accepted Christ. It was common for her to leave Hawah and I in Armah's care while she went to work and church. Ordinarily, Armah's disposition was pleasant, until one night something triggered an uncontrollable outburst. According to Mom, the devil revealed himself through Armah's eyes. Perhaps her acceptance of

Her Marriage; My Abuse

salvation stirred a spiritual storm. Regardless of what others accredit his change to, confusion, violence, and cruelty whirled into our home. When mom belted out accusations referring to Armah as "the devil," he reacted with an outburst of rage. No one likes being called a devil, but there's no excuse for how he violently pushed her. The thrust of his strength caused her to fall backward uncontrollably, she whirled around during the fall, hitting her forehead on a cabinet. The small scar above her right eye is a permanent reminder of her covenant into bondage.

Her blood loss was minimal. He tried to convince Mom that she stumbled and fell after losing balance. Nonetheless, she aggressively warned him never to hit her again. He thoroughly apologized. Later that night, she went to the emergency room to receive treatment for the minor injury. Everything checked out well, and she accepted his apology, but harbored concerns. Brothers from the church counseled Armah, but over time, his abusive behavior rekindled.

One night, we listened as Armah and Mom argued vehemently. They screamed cruel-abusive

Covenant into Bondage/ Chapter 1

words carelessly wounding each other. Suddenly, he unexpectedly slapped her across the face. The abrupt and heavy blow caused her to fall to the floor in a seated position. This time, Delpha decided to fight back. She reached and grabbed a nearby phone and broke the receiver across Armah's head. He gazed in amazement with blood streaming down his face. It was as if Mom's unexpected measure of self-defense "knocked some sense," so to speak, into Armah's head.

Although he begged her to stay, Mom immediately packed our bags and we walked out the door. Again, Armah repeatedly echoed the same promise, "I'll never do it again." Months later, he convinced her to return. Once again, life was pleasant and peaceful for a while. In fact, June 4, 1987, Mom gave birth to Arke'ya. Many days, Armah, with his foreign accent, walked around singing "I've got sunshine in the *munch* of May." His Liberian dialect added a twist of humor that made everyone in the house laugh. It seems the Roberts were finally learning what it means to be a family.

Chapter II

Way of Escape

Running From Misery

Way of Escape/ Chapter 2

God never changes, although sometimes people take drastic turns for the worst.

To our family, Armah was a man of changing faces. The nice gentleman we embraced as Dad, suddenly lost his gentle touch. The concept of family quickly dissolved. Two years of periodic and unexpected torment greeted us upon our return. We didn't know what to expect from day to day. By 1989, once again, Mom and Armah started fighting and arguing about everything.

According to Mom, nothing changed when we moved back to Virginia from Indiana. Armah pretended to be kind, and his scam worked. We were trapped in Virginia and tricked by the enemy. While reminiscing, mom says she should have ended the marriage much earlier. Hawah and Arke'ya are the only blessings she accredits to the many years of longsuffering. Those $52 Calvin Klein jeans, now faded and worn, apparently weren't worth a lifetime of abuse.

Running From Misery

Even still, she says, "I felt emotionally sick when I found out I was pregnant with Arke'ya." By day, they pretended to have the perfect marriage. By night, mom says she felt like the actress Julia Roberts in the blockbuster movie "Sleeping with the Enemy."

She says Armah made her feel as though she couldn't do anything correctly. "Nothing I did was right," she said. "And my opinions never mattered." An evil glare of revenge gazed within her squinted eyes. One evening, Mom says she repeatedly washed a long-sharp stainless-steel butcher knife as homicidal thoughts raced through her mind. "I wanted to kill him," she said. Her hands firmly gripped the knife. She thought to herself, "Perhaps this is my only way of escape." Her battered mind immediately transformed the kitchen utensil into a weapon of revenge. Suddenly, she exhaled and realized that the devil didn't just want to ruin her marriage, but his ultimate goal was to destroy her life.

They argued about everything from religion to how to do the laundry. "Hang the clothes on the line inside-out so that the sun won't fade them," Armah said. Some couples might not understand why they argued over meaningless and superficial

Way of Escape/ Chapter 2

subjects. To sum it up, I blame bitterness. Mom and Armah managed to drum-up a heated and hateful debate about everything. Everybody in our household was extremely miserable. We were prisoners behind the bars of Armah's malice. Try to imagine what it's like living an emotionally unhealthy life trapped in an environment were no adult will accept responsibility or blame for their actions.

Shortly after we moved back in with Armah, he started lashing out at me. Back then, I didn't know my biological father, in fact, I thought Armah and Mom conceived me. I desperately wanted him to love me. Regardless of how bitter some fatherless boys seem to be, most often, deep within, every male desires a dad.

I was only 8-years-old fighting against an enemy determined to destroy my future - nobody noticed the king inside the kid. Of the many cruel punishments, I despised

> **I was only 8-years-old fighting against an enemy determined to destroy my future - nobody noticed the king inside the kid.**

Running From Misery

the pain of standing on one leg for more than an hour. Meanwhile, he'd stand directly in front of me waiting on me to collapse. When my leg would give-in, he'd yell at me for failing to follow his instructions. Armah set me up for failure. Simultaneously, he used my weakness as an excuse to beat me with the metal portion of his belt-buckle. At other times, in anger he'd repeatedly slap me in the face. I was provoked to anger. My ear-drums echoed with a loud ringing sound that took hours, sometimes days, to go away.

      I wanted the nightmare to end. I was so afraid. We were living with a ticking-time-bomb waiting on his next fit of rage. Everyday it was as if I was walking on pins and needles. The worse the beatings got, the angrier I became. I even started feeling resentment toward Mom. I can still vividly picture myself as a 8-year-old defenseless boy begging her to stop him from hitting me. By this time, he'd redirected his anger from Mom toward me. I often thought to myself, "We left when he hit Mom, but why aren't we leaving now that he's beating me?" Some days he seemed pleasant, and then there were those days when he seemed to be possessed with a demon. The description of him that stands out most

Way of Escape/ Chapter 2

is Dr. Jeckel and Mr. Hide. He toyed with our emotions until we despised him.

My younger sisters spent years teaching themselves not to hate him. Personally, I don't hate him at all - my feelings toward him have always been quite difficult to explain. As the only boy in the household, I always wanted a father, and Armah was the only dad I'd ever known. My invisible biological father obviously didn't know his seed was destined for greatness, but God did. Years later, I found out that Armah isn't my dad. I located my biological father, and the sense of feeling rejected by him and Armah was to much pain for one child to bear. Sometimes I feel I have no father but God.

Meanwhile, I needed to escape, with or without Mom. I started running away. One particular morning Armah found me at a neighborhood park, and he had that evil glare in his eyes. We walked to the car, and he drove home. We immediately went into the garage. Suddenly, he started swinging a wooden plank in my direction. I dodged and ducked until he cornered me. Although physical, again the pain was unbearable, especially for an 8-year-old. He beat me with a 4x4 until my back was bruised and my

Running From Misery

arm was no longer functional. Afterward, as if nothing ever happened, he drove me to Princess Ann Elementary School. My teacher sent me to the nurse, who called Mom. In total confusion and disbelief, Mom took me to the hospital emergency room. X-rays concluded that Armah had beaten me so badly that my arm was broken.

The hospital contacted local authorities. Afterward, police and social services removed Armah from our home. The courts stipulated that he attend parenting classes. After two-months, he came home, and again, nothing changed. We welcomed home the same step-father with the same fear-provoking demon. This, I will never understand.

Finally, Mom decided that she'd rather struggle as the single mother of three. Finally, she felt as though Armah's obsession for control was not worth jeopardizing her kid's safety. In his defense, he claimed she couldn't do anything correctly. She says they argued because she wouldn't submit to his dictatorship. He never gave an excuse or an apology for his physical and verbal abuse. She despised him. He didn't care. This remained the nature of their quarrels. It takes two to argue, and they argued end-

Way of Escape/ Chapter 2

lessly. Neither Armah nor Mom are perfect, but Mom says she couldn't take anymore of the poison Armah consistently spit out. "I needed a clean break," she said. Afterward, she packed our bags and we left.

We were a long way from Gary, Indiana, and unfortunately, we didn't have anywhere to call home. Mom worked at Virginia Beech General Hospital as a patient transporter. We didn't have much. Initially, we lived in a Virginia Women's Shelter. After three months, we moved in with relatives. The courts established visitation rights between our parents. Considering that Mom desperately wanted to avoid unwanted conflict with Armah, special arrangements were made. The separation agreement instructed them to meet at the local shopping mall to allow Armah five hours with the kids every-other-Saturday.

Considering the circumstances, everything seemed to be shaping up quite well. Until Armah revealed his old habits. As a parent, he ruled and disciplined with violence. During one visit, he brutally gave Hawah an open-handed slap for saying the days of the week incorrectly. I forgave Armah repeatedly for every episode of abuse, but something

Running From Misery

inside of me changed when he hit Hawah. I felt a heated rage. My heart seemed to fall to the pit of my stomach. For a while, I hated him! We all looked to Mom for a way of escape. "I felt horrible," Mom said. "My world slipped from underneath me and I didn't know what to do." We were no longer living with Armah , but somehow he still managed to make life miserable for us.

We've forgiven Armah. Now it's clear that the solution for overcoming enemies is forgiveness. It's not always easy to do, but without forgiveness, you will always live in bondage. Forgiveness was my family's way of escape.

Way of Escape/ Chapter 2

Chapter III

Land of Promise

Destination Determines Destiny

Land of Promise/Chapter 3

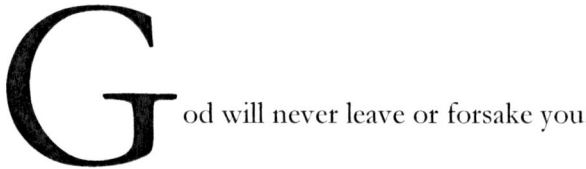od will never leave or forsake you.

I was almost 12-years old when my family finally moved back to Gary. Armah remained in Virginia, but almost every night he came to visit me in my dreams. I had countless nightmares about his abuse, but Armah is nothing more than a bad memory.

We lived in the 2100 block of Rhode Island with my grandparents. Our two-bedroom brick house was painted bright red on the front with brownish-colored-bricks on the other sides. There are two small bedrooms upstairs and three rooms in the unfinished basement. The basement is where I slept, surrounded with spider webs, cold cement walls, and concrete floors. Sometimes God wants us to pray our way to the top. I'm still praying.

During those days, I slept on a bunk bed with my cousin Chucky. We were surrounded by family, good cooking, and lots of love. There was always

Destination Determines Destiny

something interesting happening in the Lobdell household. My grandparents were used to having a crowded home because, between the two of them, they have thirteen kids. Granddaddy conceived six kids with another woman, and Grandma has six children by another man. Mom is the only child they conceived together in matrimony. The small house had always been over crowded — at the time, nine people were living under one roof. Unfortunately, four of those nine people are dead now. I came out alive.

    I attended school in Gary, Indiana at Charles R. Drew Elementary School on 21st Avenue, immediately next door to Dorie Miller Public Housing Development. We call Dorie Miller "the projects." Back then, in the projects, gangs were killing, drug addicts roamed the streets, and crime was high. Victims of poverty did anything to survive. Much about the projects hasn't changed. As a result, walking to school was a courageous journey for cousin Lew-shia (She-She) Weems and myself. Living in our neighborhood required a sense of bravery.

    I remember two guys names Bobby and

Land of Promise/Chapter 3

Booker who ridiculed us so badly that we decided to take action. Action for us meant it's time to defend ourselves by fighting. She-She is tough, and always has been. She didn't just fight girls, she wrestled with boys too. Thankfully, we are cousins, friends, and co-harts. Our relationship is unbreakable. She-She has always been more than just a cousin, she's my third sister.

She's always been lady-like, from polishing her nails and wearing Sunday dresses, to jumping double-dutch. She looks like a girl, she dresses like a woman, but she fights fearlessly. The fight with Bobby and Booker ended before the brawl ever got fierce. Unfortunately, She-She and I had countless fights lingering in paths before us.

Chucky (the-late Charles R. Snowden, III), at the time, 17-years-old, was like having a big brother. I'd iron his clothes while he'd prepare for his dates. I watched him play football for Westside High School, and then Joliet Junior College. I giggled bashfully when his girlfriends came over to our house. We fought. We laughed. We wrestled. We played. I looked up to him. Aside from Granddaddy, he was the only male-figure I had ever looked up to, at this

Destination Determines Destiny

point in my life. After everything I had gone through with Armah I needed positive male influence. Chucky and Granddaddy became my greatest inspirations.

    I spent years trying to make sense out of my past with Armah. Why did he abuse me? Why didn't he love me? Why does his voice keep ringing in my head? Questions too convoluted for a 12-year-old kid to answer. Questions too embarrassing to ask aloud. Sometimes I felt hopeless, but it's never to late to gain new hope.

    I struggled in school, and my grades were poor. After elementary, I attended Pulaski Middle School. One morning, I decided to take Granddaddy's handgun to class. I wasn't actually planning to use it. I just wanted to demonstrate a little "show and tell" so that other kids would accept and respect me. I started hanging out and trying to impress the "project kids." Everybody knew I was the preacher's grand-son who went to church Sunday after Sunday. Instead of the "church boy" reputation, I wanted to earn respect in the streets. So, I put on a façade and built a tough boy image that hindered my progress.

Land of Promise/Chapter 3

I was so caught up in building an image - something for others to worship. I wasn't certain or confident about my self-worth and self-image, so I built a make-believe image so that people would respect me. Instead of waiting to hear from God, like the children of Israel in the wilderness, I lived life based on the opinion of others.

If ever you want to discover your purpose, separate yourself from the opinions, influences, and burdens of others. God has an individual plan for each of our lives. Most people seldom arrive at the destination that God pre-determines. Sometimes, we can become so attached to family, friends, and possessions that it seems practically impossible to walk away upon God's command. Our loyalty should always be with God first, regardless of circumstances or situations.

According to scripture, Abraham's progress

Destination Determines Destiny

was delayed because he partially obeyed God (See Genesis 12 and 13). Many people do the same thing today. God says, "Go." Immediately, Christians form teams, groups, churches, clubs, and ministries. We must ask, "Why am I here; What exactly is God calling me to do?" Failing to completely follow instructions will prevent you from walking in your destiny.

Instead of taking his journey alone, as instructed by God, Abraham took his father Terah and his nephew Lot. Faith says, "You can do this thing!" Human nature says," Take a crutch; something to fall back on. Family provides a sense of support and familiarity. In fact, the Jewish culture esteems family higher than any other relationship. Perhaps these are the reasons Abraham took his family. Nonetheless, until Terah died, his father's age altered his journey, and his relationship with Lot caused an unnecessary delay. Never take extra baggage on a spiritual journey; lay aside every weight, it will slow your progress.

Ask yourself, "Do I have any extra baggage in my life?" Perhaps, as an adult, your extra baggage is the unsolicited opinions of your parents that hinders

Land of Promise/Chapter 3

your marriage. It's even possible that your extra baggage is your adult children refusing to grow up that hinders your finances. Extra baggage could be your best friend, your parents, or anything that causes you to become so attached that you refuse to let go. We have to stay focused on the promises of God. Remember, God's plan is not to harm us, but he promises to prosper us and bring us to an expected end.

Chapter IV
Forsaken
The Man In The Mirror

Forsaken/Chapter 4

God's people do not grieve the loss of loved-ones as non-believers.

Death manages to catch most people off-guard. Certainly, the death of Granddaddy came as an unexpected loss to the Baptist community of northwest Indiana. My memory serves me as if it were yesterday, when Granddaddy left forever without saying goodbye. October 2, 1994, he walked away from the world we once shared, and ascended into eternity with God. I was 14-years-old experiencing the loss of another male-role-model. The first loss was through denial, secondly divorce, and now death. I desperately needed to feel wanted. It seems the men in my life either rejected me, abused me, or died.

Granddaddy didn't have any chronic illnesses, at least none that I was made aware of anyway. I do recall him getting excessively busy during his last months with us. It's as though he knew something we didn't. His final sermon is titled, "Getting things together on the inside." In his own way, I guess he was saying "goodbye." He repaired the old-central-

The Man In The Mirror

air-conditioning-unit, built a shed, made arrangements for Deacon Fred Berry and his son Verdell to pave our driveway, and started clinging to Grandma. The Friday night before he died, Granddaddy was released from Methodist Hospital Northlake. I think he was hospitalized for a minor heart condition. Whatever it was, when he came, home everything seemed okay.

Excitement raced throughout our home Saturday morning. Granddaddy was home! Everybody was happy! Most important for me, as a 14-year-old anyway, my girlfriend was coming to church with me Sunday morning. "Granddaddy! I'm picking up Erica and bringing her to church tomorrow," I said with a sense of excitement! "You're not driving my car," he replied with sudden laughter! I explained that Mom is taking me to pick up my girlfriend and her sister Tiffany. It seems out of no where, he belted out the last seven

> **It seems out of no where, he belted out the last seven words I recall him saying, "You know, I'm so proud of you."**

Forsaken/Chapter 4

words I recall him saying, "You know, I'm so proud of you." Until then, no man ever told me he was proud of me. The next morning, Granddaddy died. Maybe God showed him my future, and just maybe those were the words that helped me cling to new hope.

We were only two blocks away from New Hope. I was in running distance away from Granddaddy. Mom turned our red station wagon onto 21st and Rhode Island, where emergency lights where flashing. An Ambulance positioned in front of the church made Mom extremely nervous. It was as if she knew exactly what happened. She instructed us to go directly to Aunt Lewisean's house. When the Ambulance left, we walked to the church not quite knowing what to expect.

Parishioners explained that Granddaddy, Pastor Lobdell, was giving closing remarks after Sunday School. In their amazement, he gently fell to the ground as though angels caught him and carried his body to the floor. Afterward, paramedics rushed him to the hospital where he was pronounced dead. Reverend James Bostic continued service in his absence. Weeks prior, Granddaddy started rotating

The Man In The Mirror

the associate ministers at the church. Rev. Bostic announced Granddaddy's home-going. I sat hunched over in the pew like an empty scarecrow. I was in shock. While seated in church, not one tear fell from either eye. When I started walking back to my aunt's house, mixed emotions whirled through my confused mind. All evening, including throughout the night, I heard Granddaddy's voice saying, "You know, I'm so proud of you."

Monday morning I cried alone. I sat on the top of the stairwell listening to the church secretary Pat Tyler console Grandma. I broke down in tears, knowing that I will never see him again in this life. I said to myself, "He's gone."

As if the loss of Granddaddy wasn't enough, Six months later, April 24, 1995, cousin Chucky was murdered. Some criminal made an unlawful entry into his Miller area apartment and shot him in the head at point-blank-range. My family and police haven't been able to determine what happen. As for me, life diminished into a distorted motionless picture of a depressed 15-year-old boy facing life alone. I didn't know my biological father because he rejected me at birth. My stepfather was violent and

Forsaken/Chapter 4

physically abusive toward me. Granddaddy's love gave me a sense of worth, and made me feel wanted, although he died way too soon. Cousin Chucky became my brother and my friend, and the devil murdered him. Here I stood, 15-years-old, lost, confused, broken, abused, rejected, lonely, and alone.

A metal folding chair, a brown 15-inch extension cord, an angry 15-year-old boy - alone I stood. I tried to commit suicide, but I failed. I couldn't take any more, so I thought. One evening, after arguing with Mom, I stormed into the basement. By this time, I'd convinced myself that Mom didn't understand the way I was feeling. I slung everything in sight trying to release a portion of the tormenting anger I felt raging within. I couldn't bear the thought of living with this emotional hole in my heart any longer. So, I grabbed a nearby extension cord.

While standing on the seat of a small chair, I tied the cord to an exposed pipe in the basement ceiling. Tears drenched my face. Panting with fear, I felt myself gasping for air, yet drowning in a whirlwind of anger and rage, but I continued. It was as if something was forcing me to tie the cord securely around my neck. I was prepared to sacrifice my life.

The Man In The Mirror

I felt miserably unwanted and lonely. After kicking the chair away, I felt myself suspended between life and death! Without a moment to spare, Mom rushed into the basement, hysterically crying while quickly removing the cord from around my bruised neck. I was on an emotional rollercoaster, Mom was the closest person to me, but I even rebelled against her. Immediately, she took me to Methodist Hospital where I was admitted into the Children's Psyche Unit for nearly 2-weeks. The face I saw each time I looked in the mirror was unbearable - I saw the reflection of a kid no one wanted, loved, or understood.

The hospital ward was unlike anything I'd experienced. Counselors, psychologists, and psychiatrists were unable to diagnose me with any known condition. Aside from anger rooted in many childhood disappointments, I was okay. Perhaps I needed a structured environment. Wake-up calls were at the same time every morning, we ate three healthy meals a day, and game time was available for those who earned the privilege. Most kids were under the influence of prescribed medication of some sort to adjust their behavior, but not me. One of my best experiences during my two-week stay was meeting a

Forsaken/Chapter 4

Gary police officer. He just so happened to be working on the homicide investigation involving the murder of cousin Chucky. Somehow, his efforts and my anticipation of vindication made me feel somewhat hopeful.

According to staff clinicians, nothing was wrong with me - they gave no diagnoses. Maybe, like so many other youth, all I needed was a little hope. Unfortunately, my failed attempt at suicide left others concerned. My not-well-thought-out, or rash and impulsive suicidal decision, caused concerns that forced physicians to imprison me in a facility with dirty showers and limited freedom. The humility and embarrassment of being on a hospital mental ward stalked me for years.

God knew my ultimate destiny, and he was preparing me for my purpose and assignment. I am confident that it is the life outside the pulpit that lends anointing to powerful preachers, not the inspirational messages, popularity, fancy words, or big titles. When everything is said and done, what is your image of the man in the mirror. God has a way of showing us who we really are - great or small, good or bad.

Chapter V

Searching for Identity

Manmade mistakes,
God made miracles

Searching for Identity/Chapter 5

God creates everyone with purpose, even when mistakes and misfortunes make life feel meaningless.

Sixteen years of my life quickly passed. High school always remained a struggle for me. In an effort to avoid the violence at Roosevelt High School, Mom enrolled me into Calumet Baptist during the ninth and tenth grades. Afterward, she transferred me to Wirt High School in the miller area of Gary. Perhaps I should have stayed at Calumet Baptist.

Transferring to Wirt High School during my junior year was clearly a mistake. I spent most of my time trying to fit in, adjusting to the surroundings, and investing energy fighting enemies and smoking marijuana. Getting high became second nature for me. Little did I know, I'd suffer the consequences of my actions as time progressed. Wirt was nothing like Calumet Baptist School in Hobart. The kids are physically larger, the school is much bigger, and Wirt's student population is astronomical, compared

Manmade Mistakes, God Made Miracles

to Calumet Baptist. Wirt seemed to have more African American kids than any school I'd attended. I found myself aimlessly drifting, totally lost, and desperately trying to be cool.

The violence Mom tried sheltering me from, must have followed me to Wirt. Two guys, whom I knew very little about, tried ganging up on me. The brawl started because the guys were jealous of a girl that supposedly liked me. Out of no where, a group of guys intervened and stood up for me. I later discovered that they are all from one family. Simon (Lil' Sam), Keenan, and Bruce, made up the Lillie brothers. Also, their cousins Gerrick Williams (BoBo), Otheniel Mahone (O.T.), and Kenneth Butler (Mann), came to my rescue. Lil' Sam and myself soon became best friends, and his family became my family. They accepted me.

During lunch hours we walked the surge area, when in trouble we fought together, and we made the best of every weekend. From street basketball, baseball, football, bowling, movies, and dances, we always managed to find something exciting to do! Although I gained the support of a group of friends, I still felt the need to earn acceptance from others.

Searching for Identity/Chapter 5

    I was the only one out of the group that smoked Marijuana daily. During lunch hour, I searched until I found some buddies to smoke weed with. I still wanted to be cool, as opposed to just having a church boy reputation. Eventually, my desire to fit in turned into an addiction. I started craving the euphoric and relaxed feeling I acquired from inhaling drugs. I wanted it more and more. I used my lunch money and any spare change I got to get a quick high. Sometimes I'd share and allow other kids to smoke for free, when I didn't have money, they returned the favor.

    My grades were suffering horribly. I never achieved more than a "D" average. I was distracted by thoughts of being normal, fitting in, and gaining acceptance. Meanwhile, my grades ranged from "C" to "F." By the end of the school year, I moved on as a senior, but my credits reflected that I was a half year behind.

    At age seventeen, Mom allowed me to live with the Lillie family in the Miller area of Gary. We didn't live in the district where I attended school, so, I relocated to their home. Mom purchased groceries to help out and show gratitude. No matter how

Manmade Mistakes, God Made Miracles

much people invested into my life, my behavior seemed to get worse. My entire senior year I encountered fight-after-fight. Trouble seemed to be my middle name, and it was nothing I was proud of. Sometimes, administrators suspended me and other times my mischievous behavior went without notice. My surroundings changed, but my attitude remained destructive.

Unfortunately, I was unable to participate in senior graduation. I was certain I didn't have enough credit-hours to receive my diploma, but I wanted to celebrate with my classmates, and complete my studies during the summer. After getting caught in a fight involving schoolmates, the principal prevented me from coming back on campus. Of my group of close friends, Lil Sam and I were the only seniors. Unfortunately, my campus restrictions prevented me from supporting his graduation. Wouldn't you know it, Lil Sam graduated and became a Gary Police Officer. When we first met, he was defending me, and now he's protecting the entire city of Gary.

Refusing to drop out of school, I earned the remainder of the my credits at Portage Adult Education. I waited until the following year and walked

Searching for Identity/Chapter 5

across the stage with other adult graduates. My mother was the only family member present. I felt somewhat discouraged by the lack of attendance, but little did I know, I'd stand on platforms and pulpits with even larger audiences for the rest of my life.

After high school, life seemed to have no real meaning. I wandered aimlessly from job-to-job. I didn't really want to work, but as an adult living under Mom's roof, I had to. My life was drifting like a gusting wind that whirls through before a tornado. I was practicing a lifestyle of premarital sex, treating women like trash, and selfishly ignoring the importance and power of God.

My heart was empty and my life was void of purpose. As a result, I searched for physical pleasures to satisfy my carnal desires. An idle mind is truly the devil's workshop. Satan drew me into a filthy life of lust, until I became reacquainted with an old friend by the name of Tiffany Hammonds. Tiffany also attended Wirt High School, we dated for a while, but our courtship didn't amount to anything. Although, we shared a lot in common. Our high school relationship seemed no different from any other teenage fling. As adults, we re-evaluated our relationship.

For a while, I thought she understood me. Like myself, she grew up in her grandfather's church - Miracle Temple Church of God in Christ in Gary. As teenagers, we were able to relate unlike any other relationship I'd shared. She supported me at age-18 when I preached my first sermon. Our relationship evolved around religion, church, and God. By age 19, we were engaged to be married. Unfortunately, I hadn't totally recovered from my past. Anger and rage ruled in my life. It seems I was transforming into the man who abused me for years. In a sense, Armah seemed to have resurrected in me. The only difference is I didn't physically abuse the women in my life. I kept the violence in the streets, but my uncontrollable anger and verbal abuse remained an issue.

> **Most men need to be heard, I was crying out from within, and Monique listened and related to everything I felt.**

Our young engagement was impregnated

Searching for Identity/Chapter 5

with promise, but Tiffany aborted our union, after I polluted it with arguments. Her decision only caused us to argue more. After I got involved in another relationship, she claimed that we'd never broken up. As a young man, I felt as though we did. Actions speak louder than words. When men and women argue constantly, their covenant of agreement becomes distorted, and the true meaning of relationship is lost. In part, Tiffany helped shape me into the minister I am today. While dating her, I gained a passion for volunteering in the church. My love and servitude for God's people remained, however, our relationship changed, and I moved on.

Less than a year later, at age 20, my life took a sudden shift. I received my minister's license, and Serrita Monique Kendrick returned to New Hope. I was sitting in church minding my own business, but her beauty was unavoidable. She'd recently relocated back to Gary from Houston, Texas. I nervously made my "preacher-boy approach." That Sunday morning, my childhood crush quickly evolved into an adult love affair.

Initially, Monique and I talked countless hours over the telephone. While Tiffany and I

Manmade Mistakes, God Made Miracles

shared a lot of similar church experiences, Monique shared my pain. Naturally, I was drawn to the woman that seemed to make my anguish go away. From sun-down to sun-up, we shared our struggles, our challenges, and our deepest hurts - secrets we promised never to tell. She gave me an opportunity to pour out my heart in a way I'd never done before. Most men need to be heard, I was crying out from within, and Monique listened and related to everything I felt.

In addition to the struggles we had in common, she was soft spoken, beautiful, understanding, and seemingly everything I thought I wanted in a wife. She dressed classy, seemed very caring, and she communicated as though she was really into me. It appeared as though she worshipped God from her heart. We even studied the Bible together. Unlike past relationships, I wanted Monique, and only Monique.

She had previously ventured into a world of darkness, but it was that world that caused us to relate so well. Considering my dark childhood, although in different ways, we had both been victimized, belittled and wounded. We did what we

Searching for Identity/Chapter 5

thought people in love are suppose to do. We looked beyond one another's faults, as much as we knew how to anyway. We talked about the Word of God, went to church regularly, talked on the phone nightly, and slipped into sin frequently. We justified our debauchery by saying, "People make mistakes." We considered our sexual escapades just that, mistakes. We repented and moved on. As far as we were concerned, sex was a part of falling in love. We were both immature, ignorant, and unlearned during those days.

November 2000, I was 21-years-old, and we eloped. Nobody knew but us. We drove to Crown Point and went to the Justice of Peace. We said our vows, and promised to spend the rest of our lives together. We had no clue what marriage was all about. We only knew how much we wanted to feel accepted, loved, and unashamed forever. Our secret remained safe. We both went back to separate homes, living with our parents.

Our intentions were pure, we loved God, we couldn't resist one another, and we decided not to live a life of sin, debauchery, or even one overshadowed by "frequent mistakes." What's done

Manmade Mistakes, God Made Miracles

in darkness will soon come to the light. December 14, 2000, I was involved in a horrible car accident. My friend Curtis Griffin was driving, Anthony (Tiny) Owens was in the back seat, and I was in the front passenger seat. We were merging onto the Broadway entry ramp of I-94, when we hit a patch of black ice. The car spent around into oncoming traffic, slid underneath a semi-truck, and slung into a nearby ditch. Blood running from my temple down the right side of my face drove me into a state of shock. I recall one police officer asking, "What's your favorite sport?" I replied, "Jesus." "What's your favorite color," he asked. "Jesus," I repeated. Afterward, I was taken to Northlake Methodist Hospital and admitted for three days. As my faithful wife, Monique seldom left my side. Considering that no one else knew, they questioned her zealous involvement and felt as though she was overly concerned.

    The pressure continued to build. So, we told. Through a phone conversation we told her dad, Leon Kendricks. He seemed extremely disappointed. In anger, he demanded that she pack her bags and get out - "Go be with your husband," he screamed! Afterward, for about six months, we lived in Mom's basement. The same basement where I tried to com-

Searching for Identity/Chapter 5

mit suicide. The same basement where my deceased cousin Chucky and I shared bunk-beds. The same basement where I sat crying on the stairwell when Pat Tyler consoled Grandma. For me, nothing but bad things always seemed to spiral from that basement.

We moved into a building on Gary's 5th and Taft, afterward, we discovered that it was condemned. As a result, we moved again, and found a home in Westbrook Apartments. We both understood and accepted the idea of humble beginnings. Unfortunately, the more stress we acquired, the more we argued. We disagreed and argued infrequently while dating, but nothing compared to now. Every little thing evolved into a major conflict, just as it did with Armah and Mom.

When we argued, we aimed to hurt one another, so, we lashed out with the secrets we knew about each other's past. We never hit one another, although once, she did shove my face, and during another escalated episode, I aggressively grabbed both of her arms trying to put fear in her heart. I often tell people our break-up was my fault, although neither of us were prepared for marriage. Somehow, lies and rumors spread that I physically abused

Manmade Mistakes, God Made Miracles

Monique, perhaps in the fit of a heated rage my voice posed threats, but I never beat her, seriously. Unfortunately, abuse is all we knew, and it became the centerpiece of our relationship.

Some people, especially my family, say Monique intended to harm me from the beginning, but that's not true. I still believe in her innocence. Much like myself, she's been wounded from the events of her past. Life can leave some horrible scars. The car accident left a clearly visible 5-inch blemish on my face. Many people think my elbow scar came from the accident also, but it didn't. I dove for a loose basketball at Calumet Baptist School, and my elbow-bone snapped. I had 42-stiches as a child, although recovering from emotional injuries is far more difficult than physical wounds. Scars heals within weeks, but the heart requires more time and treatment for a full recovery. Believe me, I should know, I've overcome both.

In February 2002, Monique and I separated. I moved out and returned to Mom's basement. In March, we learned she was pregnant. We desperately tried working through our problems, but we needed help from God. Instead of praying more, we argued

Searching for Identity/Chapter 5

worse. Finally, we gave up.

We filed for divorce in June 2002, but Indiana courts wouldn't pass the motion because Monique was pregnant. Leon Carl Kendricks was born November 13, immediately following, our disgraceful divorce was final.

Chapter VI

Torn into a Million Pieces

Consequences of Covenant Breaking

Torn into a Million Pieces/Chapter 6

God says, "It's better not to make a vow, than to make it and break it."

November 2002, I was nearing depression. My recent divorce caused me to feel overwhelmed by defeat. It merely represented another public failure. For the second time in life, I felt like giving up. The enemy started getting the best of my emotions. It seemed almost impossible for me to piece my life back together. I lacked stability. I needed help, and I didn't have anywhere to turn.

Circumstances continued spiraling downward. My inability to keep a job prevented me from financially caring for my newborn son. Infants need pampers, milk, clothes, hygiene products, toys and time. I was inconsistent with everything except spending time. Being that I quit my jobs so frequently, I had more than enough time to spare. I despised my failures; with a broken heart I cried many tears on Mom's shoulders.

I wanted the respect of a man, but I lacked

Consequences of Covenant Breaking

adult responsibility. As a tenant of the Lobdell residence, I was forced to submit to Mom's rules. My life seemed to remain the same since childhood. I didn't possess any defining characteristics of a man, aside from physical anatomy. I felt like half-man and half-boy. Sadness always hailed around me, overshadowing my countenance.

More than anything or anyone, I blame myself. I take full responsibility for my secret marriage and public divorce, poor work ethics, and irresponsible parenting. Although I must admit, simply seeing my ex–wife left me feeling like a failure through and through. She became a mental image of another ruined attempt at life. The devil cornered me into believing that my entire existence is a mistake.

Monique always felt as though my last name meant nothing. Considering the circumstances, some might agree, but I'm proud of who I am. Names do not define successful people. Great legacies are gained, not given. My biological father's surname is Akins, my step-father's name is Roberts, and I am of the blood lineage of the Lobdell family. Monique's decision could have spiraled from many reasons. Perhaps she didn't believe in me, maybe she wanted

Torn into a Million Pieces/Chapter 6

to spite me, some say, she aimed to regain the support of her dad, or then again, it's possible that she couldn't see the king inside the kid. Either way, I understand, because it took years before I gained a sense of individual identity. Now, I know who I am.

Back then, she used my adopted-name as an excuse to give my son her father's full name, Leon Carl Kendricks - we call him Carl. Unfortunately, I didn't have the strength to fight back. "Just forget it," is how I often felt.

> Regardless of her unknown motivation, Monique's decision felt like a heart-piercing dagger, but Carl's love raptures me.

It's weird, because he's my firstborn son, and mirrors my image, but lacks my name. The removal of my last name represented Satan's effort to invalidate my existence as Carl's father. Regardless of her unknown motivation, Monique's decision felt like a heart-piercing dagger, but Carl's love raptures me.

Initially, I was limited to supervised visita-

-82-

Consequences of Covenant Breaking

tions at her house only, until we went to custodial court. Afterward, I was awarded supervised visitations at Mom's house. Although I have no criminal records or history of misconduct, illegal activity, or child neglect, Mom was ordered to be present whenever Carl came to visit. This too, remained another battle I had no strength to fight. Remember, God's strength is made perfect in weakness. I remember sitting in the Gary City Court room feeling as though my parental rights were being violated. Before I could respond, God said, "Hold your peace."

Initially, I couldn't understand why the white-female-judge wouldn't give me visitation rights. Later, I begin to realize that our society gives limited rights to unwed fathers. Monique insisted on painting a cruel and vicious image that made me appear unfit and unstable during the custodial hearing. I questioned her about suspicions of gaining negative influence from our pastor. I needed an answer considering that it was becoming increasingly difficult to serve as his amour bearer with thoughts of him having ruined my family. She denied it. Being that I couldn't do anything about his alleged manipulation, I accepted her confession at face value. I thought to myself, perhaps my speculations are a tad bit judgmental. Especially considering that her impeccable beauty made me feel insecure from time to time. I blamed myself, apologized, and felt guilty for even making the accusation.

About two years later, according to the Post Tribune newspaper, they conceived a child during an adulterous affair, as a result, he was ousted from our New Hope church family. Immediately afterward, he started a new church, divorced his wife, and married my son's mother. Due to a tragic episode involving possible mistreatment of their newborn, social services designated me as Carl's custodial parent. I continued holding my peace for two years, and God fought my battle. My custodial challenges with Carl taught me something about our Lord: nothing shall separate us from the love of the father.

Although I desperately found myself trying to live for Christ, my divorce rendered consequences that tore my life into a million pieces. I felt lonely, and I needed a friend. Suddenly, *out of no where*, came Anita Stone. It was as though I took a deep breath, exhaled, and then thought to myself, "she's so beautiful." With hair stretching down her back, a smile that strengthens me, and eyes that sparkle like the

Consequences of Covenant Breaking

moonlight, Anita slowly took my breath away. She's a mature woman of faith. We started off as friends, until I started thinking I could have a second chance at love. I saw her as an opportunity to prove that I can maintain a lasting relationship. Most importantly, she believes in me. I wanted to make things right within my heart, and she had all the ingredients for a successful relationship.

From November 2002 until January 2003, we were no more than platonic friends. We talked about life, love, and struggles on a daily basis. She has an angel for a daughter name Giara Stevenson. Together, we were a small family. I enjoy her presence like no other woman I've ever known. She made me feel brand new. My weakness overtook me in January; we crossed the lines of love. We both felt uncomfortable, and decided to go our separate ways. Two months later, I received an unexpected phone call, "I know we said we shouldn't talk anymore, but we're not going to be able to

> Sieon, Jr. makes me want to give radical praises to God, because his birth rekindled my joy.

Torn into a Million Pieces/Chapter 6

do that, I'm pregnant."

Again, it seemed as though my heart fell into the pit of my stomach. I sat on the phone speechless. "Hello," she echoed repeatedly. I didn't know what to say or do. I was devastated. No matter how much I tried to do right, I kept failing. Premarital sex was a bad and immoral decision, and it seemed to be the same trap Satan kept using to derail me. In addition to facing the consequences of my wrong actions, I was afraid that people would reject me, fail to forgive, or label me a loser. When we disobey God's word, we have to deal with the unwanted consequences. Consequences build character. At the time, I refused to accept or acknowledge another child born into my unwed situation. I never intended to insult or hurt Anita, but considering all the failures of my past, what was I to do? Although the answer to that question seemed simple, I specialized in making wrong choices. For months, I lived life as though that phone call never happened. Although my actions unequivocally appeared heartless, Anita soon learned the truth about my feelings.

I continued ministering almost weekly throughout the city of Gary. I preached and sang

Consequences of Covenant Breaking

praises everywhere churches invited me. During the United Methodist Annual Unity Service at Lake Michigan, I met a Post-Tribune correspondent named Anthony KaDarrell Thigpen. He understood friendship and loyalty in a way I'd never experienced it. We developed a relationship that allowed me to open-up and trust him. I told him everything about my life, with the exception of Anita's coming arrival. Some things I belted out, others I gradually explained as months passed. I was extremely reluctant to tell him about the young lady I'd currently impregnated. I began to look up to him, months passed, he wrote a couple of newspaper articles featuring me, and we developed an unbreakable-brotherly-bond. He soon became my best friend, my only true friend, and I grew to love him as one would a biological brother. This time, I didn't want anything to ruin what we shared, not death or denial, and especially not another one of my failures.

He taught me the value of humility, and October 7, 2003, God honored my lowliness. Sieon Roberts, Jr. was born on the morning of my birthday. We share the same name, the same facial features, and the same birth date. Sieon, Jr. makes me want to give radical praises to God, because his birth rekin-

Torn into a Million Pieces/Chapter 6

dled my joy. Sieon means praise, because of him, I exalt the Lord, because his joy is my strength.

Most people spend a lifetime without even understanding what friendship means. I've experienced it first hand. KaDarrell is Sieon's godfather. Our relationship continues to blossom, sometimes it even feels spiritual. Unlike other men in my life, I feel certain that he's here to stay. He provides me with a sense of stability. In addition, his prayers for me are rich and heartfelt. KaDarrell helped me put the pieces of my life back together. Although he'd say it was God, I know that God used him as a vessel to turn my life around.

Chapter VII

Humility, Honor, and Hope

Let The Meek Rejoice

Humility, Honor, and Hope/Chapter 7

God forbids us from thinking more highly of ourselves than we ought.

Humility is sacrificing your time, treasures, and talents, despite your own feelings, in order to act how God wants you to. Humility is born out of spiritual maturity, it's a characteristic that's tough to acquire. Loving people who despitefully misuse you is clearly not easy. Facing emotionally overwhelming situations and maintaining a Christ-like attitude requires a sense of selflessness and maturity.

Most of my mistakes, from drinking alcohol and smoking marijuana to impregnating women outside of marriage caused public humiliation. Also, a painful divorce, following our short matrimony, high school failures, and sporadic-meaningless relationships made me appear less than a man. I often asked myself, "How will I cope with the judgmental glares of others?" I've learned that humility is measured based on how we handle ourselves when a demand is placed on our faith.

Let The Meek Rejoice

Either pride or humility will accompany everyone of our actions. My countless mistakes taught me how to take the low road in life. Humility the road least traveled, although it's an honorable journey. When I humbled myself, God exalted me; when I faced my public failures with courage, the Lord anointed me to preach and sing. "Humble yourselves in the sight of the Lord and he shall lift you up," (James 4:10). As a result of humbling myself, I found favor with God; when I accepted responsibility for my actions, I started walking in honor and taking ministry seriously. Suddenly, doors started opening. It seemed as if some doors appeared in the midst of thin air. When we walk in humility, God shows up *out of no where*, so to speak.

Suddenly, churches, pastors, and associates started asking me to speak and preach at events, conferences, and miscellaneous services. This is one of my most humbling experiences, although I wanted to just run away and leave my mistakes behind, God helped me to confront them.

I continued singing and directing my New Hope church choir every Sunday, Wednesday, and during rehearsals. Directing placed me in the face of

Humility, Honor, and Hope/Chapter 7

my former father-in-law, Mr. Kendrick, who worked as our minister of music. I respected him, which made me feel comfortable. And he handled his public responsibilities with grace. We worked well together, at the amazement of naysayers; eyes squinted in confusion and whispering questions marked many rehearsals. Some gossipers asked with suspicion, "Is everything okay between you two?" Oftentimes, hoping to find a reason to spread bad news.

Mr. Kendrick and I shared a relationship that was no different from any of the other choir members. We were a traditional church choir. While marching into the sanctuary, with hands clapping and feet stomping, our voices echoed throughout our newly constructed nearly 1200-seat facility. With smiling faces, we sang to the glory of God. During those days, three of my favorite songs were "Changed," "I am Redeemed," and "All in His hands." I was finally learning to give my entire life to God, even my disappointments, heartaches, and failures.

In addition to preaching amongst huge congregations, despite my public disgrace, and working

Let The Meek Rejoice

hand-in-hand with Mr. Kendrick, I also faced another humiliating challenge. Imagine standing before a congregation of about 300 parishioners confessing your sins to members who only know you as a licensed minister. Remember, according to popular belief, ministers aren't expected to make mistakes. Although we know this isn't true. If ever I'd accepted responsibility for my mistakes before, it was October 2003. "I'm standing before you all because many of you have watched me grow. You've been with me through ups and downs, and because of this I respect you. Recently, I made a mistake. As a leader in the ministry, I feel the need to address the church and apologize to my pastor, fellow ministers, and our church as a whole. I am an unwed father, and for this, I am sorry." While I was yet repenting, God's presence embraced me. Tears fell from my eyes, many members immediately assembled around me with hugs and a welcomed display of love. God was transforming my humility into honor.

    Humility isn't always easy to display, it demands modesty. It's a result of being overlooked, stepped on, and admitting guilt even when you're not necessarily wrong. Although personally, I was trespassing across territory that should have been con-

Humility, Honor, and Hope/Chapter 7

fronted long before. Among many things, confronting my failures taught me that without humility, it's impossible to totally dedicate your life to Christ. Otherwise, we only give God what we think is worthwhile, when in fact, he uses our weaknesses to build character. God says, "Let the weak say I am strong."

God's strength is made perfect in weakness, according to II Corinthians 12:9. News continued traveling about God's favor in my life. Although I felt unworthy, others felt God's anointing whenever I delivered a message. Now I understand that I've been given special power from God to minister his word and sing his praises. I realize now more than ever, that the life of a clergyman outside the pulpit is what empowers us to preach in the pulpit. Otherwise, without accepting responsibility for our actions and trying to do better, we minister in vain. Nobody is perfect, that's why humility is a costly commodity for Christians - we need it in order to look at the man in the mirror. Otherwise, arrogance and selfishness will prevent us from seeing ourselves as others do. Our weaknesses are constant reminders that our strengths, abilities, and anointing comes from God. This is why it's okay to accept and acknowledge our flaws.

Let The Meek Rejoice

Years prior, when I was 19-years-old, still dating Tiffany, I wandered from the safety of all I'd ever known at New Hope. For about one year I found myself in the wilderness. I was searching for something more. I soon discovered that certain something is God's anointing. Spiritually speaking, I became a man under the tutelage of Pastor Terry Garmon of Greater New Zion Apostolic. My Baptist background became saturated with Pentecostal influence. Pastor Garmon taught me about the purpose of the Holy Ghost. I'd already received him into my life, although I was unlearned. During my short stay at his church, he embraced me, trained me in scripture, imparted wisdom and anointing, and personally gave me the strength to handle rejection.

A minor disagreement caused Pastor Garmon to take away my ministerial rights. We disagreed, he maintained his perspective, and so do I. I felt misunderstood. He says he felt ignored. I was accused of being disobedient, and instead of reasoning with me, I felt as though he condemned me. More than anything, I felt rejected, but rejection put me on the path of walking in God's promises. For this, I will always love Pastor Garmon. The pain of rejection is part of the preparation I needed for my destiny. Soon after,

Humility, Honor, and Hope/Chapter 7

I returned to New Hope with new hope.

The Bible says, "Hope that is seen is not hope." The things I used to hope for have come to pass. Now I have new hope, a new outlook, and new vision.

Also when I was nineteen, Nikia Hammond-Blakely, sister of my former fiancé Tiffany, allowed me to sing backup for her group. During this time in my life, I was exposed to the local music industry. I sang with groups like Truly Anointed, Redeemed, Celestial Voices, and I directed Unity Youth Choir. As time progressed, I met a Elder Brandon Jacobs, we developed an awesome friendship. Friends are something I lacked, because my adult life had not granted me the opportunity to master the ministry of friendship.

More than friendship, or any other relationship life has to offer, deep within I hoped to marry again. Only this time, I wanted it to last forever. The only problem is that I didn't know if Anita and I were in love, or merely parenting a child together. Either way, what we shared felt really special. Even still, I remained confused, seeking love from two women at

Let The Meek Rejoice

the same time. They were both frustrated because the truth is I didn't deserve either of them, at the time. Although, Anita found herself fighting to preserve the family structure we were building.

This was the first time a woman actually put up a struggle to keep me in her life. This is why Anita's actions often resulted in an argument. She had her hands on what she wanted, and I only knew what I hoped for. She understood me, and I misunderstood her. I was at fault, and I pointed the blame at her.

Things changed. When KaDarrell found out about the other woman that I'd been hiding in secret, as usual, he held me accountable. I realized again that having him as a friend is worthwhile, and that with him I have nothing to hide. The Bible says, "Love covers a multitude of sins." His actions proved that he loves me.

To everybody's surprise, Anita and I abruptly decided to marry. Some people questioned our motives, others disagreed with our hasty decision, but it seems everyone supported us during our ceremonious occasion. Our pastor facilitated the ceremony, we said our vows, and June 14, 2004, and life took on new meaning. KaDarrell and his fiancé Clara, selflessly coordinated our reception.

Before the year ended, my ex-wife alleged that our pastor impregnated her. This is when articles appeared in local newspapers and rumors spread quickly. Although he initially denied the allegations, the Deacons Board ousted him. For one year, New Hope went without a church pastor. Chairman Fred Berry and the Deacon's Board made sure the church affairs were handled thoroughly. We worshipped in a newly-constructed-$2 million facility in need of a new pastor. It wasn't long before the church came into agreement. This entire account reminds me of King David, and how Samuel anointed him King while Saul was still in authority. I already knew God's plan for my life, and I watched in amazement as he carried it out.

January 26, 2005, Anita gave birth to Jeremiah Clarence Roberts. Although most people fail to realize it, names have great meaning. Clarence is the first name of my beloved grandfather. A man that would spread his suit coat on concrete surfaces and slide on his back underneath his member's stalled

Let The Meek Rejoice

automobiles. A man who allowed homeless members to reside in his home until they found shelter of their own. To me, Clarence identifies our son as God's servant. Jeremiah is the prophet of whom God said, "Before I formed you in your mother's womb, I knew you," (Jeremiah 1:5). In the Hebrew language the name Jeremiah means to lift up, throw, establish, and exalt. November 2005, the year of Jeremiah's birth, members came into agreement. They voted to have me serve as pastor of New Hope Missionary Baptist Church. My youngest son, Jeremiah gives me strength, he lifts up the Lobdell legacy, and he represents the power of hope fulfilled.

> **Jeremiah gives me strength, he lifts up the Lobdell legacy, and he represents the power of hope fulfilled.**

"Faith is the substance of things hoped for and the evidence of things not seen," (Hebrews 11:1). God always manages to fulfill my hopes; it's like I'm living a dream. Although God is exalting me, I am committed to walking in humility, and he continues to honor me with divine favor. Humility, honor, and

Humility, Honor, and Hope/Chapter 7

hope are a combination of three attributes that cause me to rejoice with exceedingly great joy. Now, as the 26-year-old senior pastor of one of the greatest flocks in God's kingdom, I have new hope because of *New Hope*.

Chapter VIII

Power of Forgiveness

Faith Without Forgiveness Fails

Power of Forgiveness/Chapter 8

God's hand is resting on my life, because I am a giver.

Non-believers think that when they put their offering in the church baskets they are giving to the preacher. On the other hand, people of faith are confident that God is the recipient of their financial gifts. According to the Bible, God promises to open the windows of heaven and pour out more blessings than we're able to receive when we tithe. Also, when we give, he promises to multiply our harvest and cause us to find favor with men.

It's unfortunate that most people forfeit their 30, 60, and 100 fold blessings because they fail to forgive. I've discovered that God is not interested in our financial sacrifices when we are holding grudges against others. It's impossible to give without forgiveness.

"Fore" and/or "For" is the Latin root that suggests "something must come first." For example: before, forethought, foremost, and most importantly

Faith Without Forgiveness Fails

forgive. In other words, before you give anything to God something is required of you first. It's called "forgiveness." God says make peace with others before you lay your sacrifice on the altar. Even more profound, he says he will not forgive us, if we do not forgive one another. Hence, when you bring your financial gifts to God, if you have unforgiveness in your heart, your offering will not produce an expected result.

Do you know anyone with a dream deferred? These are people that seem to possess all the right ingredients to succeed, but they've been stuck at the same spot for years. They might even be faithful in ministry, tithers, sacrificial givers, Bible scholars, and people of great character, but I assure you something is missing. God's word is true. God cannot lie. God says he wants us to prosper even as our souls prosper. Since God wants us to prosper, why are so many believers still living in lack? In many cases, the answer is unforgiveness.

> **Since God wants us to prosper, why are so many believers still living in lack?**

Power of Forgiveness/Chapter 8

When we forgive those who despitefully misuse us, we restore them into a position of favor. Just as God has done for us - we've obtained favor because of Jesus' act of forgiveness. True forgiveness reconciles enemies as friends regardless of what they've done. We too, were once enemies of the cross, but God reconciled, or drew us back to himself through Christ. Now, he calls us his friends. Oftentimes, modern day Christians claim to forgive, but instead, they move on, move away, divorce, separate, ignore, and overlook wrongdoers. If we expect God to accept our sacrifices, we must first secure them to the altar. The altar is where God evaluates the sincerity of our hearts.

Forgiving wrongdoers is never an easy task. I forgave Armah for how his abuse built strongholds that affected my childhood, my family, and my marriages. I also forgave him for failing at fatherhood. I even forgave Mom for staying with him after he violently broke my arm. Her commitment to marriage made me feel as though my safety and existence were worthless. By staying with Armah for as long as she did, it taught me that marriage is something worth working at.

Faith Without Forgiveness Fails

Whether through premarital sex, divorce or abortion, I forgave the women in my life who allowed me to degrade them and myself.

As far as the men in my life are concerned, I forgave my biological father for being absent throughout my life. I forgave Granddaddy for dying when I needed him most. I forgave my ousted pastor for serving as a prototype of King Saul while I served as his armor bearer. I forgave my spiritual mentor for teaching me rejection through personal example. I forgave my ex-father-in-law for missing out on an opportunity to father me. More than anyone, I forgave myself for ignoring the power of God and hindering divine progress by committing countless and careless sins and mistakes.

Many people fail to understand why God demonstrates his divine favor on my life. It's because I live a lifestyle of giving, and this way of living starts with forgiveness. Perhaps by acknowledging and confessing my own mistakes, I am able to empathize with the weaknesses of others. I find it somewhat easy to forgive others, because I've received such immeasurable forgiveness myself.

Power of Forgiveness/Chapter 8

Christians who fail to forgive others are merely saying, "Your sins are worse than mine," or "When I asked God to forgive me I didn't think what I'd done was really that bad." At some time in the past, we were all sinners until we accepted our Lord and Savior. As freely as we have received forgiveness, we should give it.

Most interesting, although forgiveness restores favor to wrongdoers, it serves a greater purpose for the person doing the forgiving. When we forgive, we are empowered to fulfill our purpose in life. Consider Christ, who became the savior of the world when he forgave our sins. His forgiveness reconciles us into friendship and favor with God. Afterward, the scripture says, he ascended with all power.

Chapter IX
Legacy of Leadership

I Am Born To Preach The Gospel

Legacy of Leadership/Chapter 9

God's word is like fire shut up in my bones, without question, I was born to preach God's word.

Now, I am a new creature in Christ. Among many witnesses, my testimony continues to flourish and reflect God's favor. I take no glory for God's wondrous works, because without him, I am nothing. Although, when we suffer with him, he allows us to share in his manifested glory.

There's a story in the Old Testament book of Daniel that explains how God responds to people who refuse to give up. The scenario is about three Hebrew boys who were taken captive by Babylon. In effort for King Nebuchadnezzar to strip them of their God-given roots and distort their spiritual identity, they were given pagan names. Hananiah, which means "Yahweh is gracious," was changed to Shadrach. Meshach's Hebrew name is Mishael, which means "Who is what God is." Azariah means "Yahweh has helped," although his name was changed to Abednego which is to say "servant."

I Am Born To Preach The Gospel

These three boys came out of the lineage of Judah, which means praise.

Praise is what God's people should produce. The devil wants to take our praise captive in order to destroy our spiritual identity. I repeat, the devil wants to steal your praise. The battle has gotten so bad that most churches have "cheer leaders." Some one has to pump-up the congregation every service, because believers refuse to praise God unless they are primed. The devil is attacking our praise. He wants us to think we are nothing more than our most recent mistake, but not so. We are new creatures. We are not liars, adulterers, fornicators, backbiters, thieves, murderers, or anything else the devil tries to deceive us into thinking we are. We are servants of the most high God, more than conquerors, and overcomers in Christ.

As the story continues, Nebuchadnezzar ordered the Hebrew captives to bow down to a pagan image. When they refused, the fiery furnace was turned up seven times hotter than usual. Even still, they would not bow. We have to be more like the Hebrew boys when it comes to our praise. No matter what we're going through, our praise is a weapon of faith - God takes residence in our praises. When they were thrown into the furnace, they were not harmed. The Bible says there was a forth image in the fire that looked like the son of God. When we suffer for God, we share in his glory. Remember, God inhabits our praises. Wherever we praise him, he will show up!

For years, I never understood why life seemed to beat me senseless. Now I understand that God has been trying to reveal his glory to me since childhood. The apostle Paul said, "The sufferings of this present time are not worthy to be compared to the glory that shall be revealed in us." I could not have said it better!

> **David said, "Thou prepares a table before me in the presence of my enemies."**

The Bible teaches us to live a lifestyle of sacrificial praise. Now that I've matured in Christ, I understand something profound about the principles of God surrounding praise and worship. Obedience is better than sacrifice. In the Old Testament book of II Samuel, the Israelites were carrying the ark of

I Am Born To Preach The Gospel

the covenant back to its rightful place, and rejoicing and praising God. In the heat of the moment, so to speak, Uzzah noticed the ark slipping from the carrying cart and put out his hand to steady it. Immediately, the Bible says, God struck him dead for touching the holy object. Why? God had already informed his people how sacred the ark is, and identified those who should and should not touch it. I've learned that our praise is worthless without a lifestyle of obedience. Praise and worship should never be approached without reverence. The scripture says, "Obedience is better than sacrifice."

Instead of recognizing that God has a purpose for everyone, many people disrespect God by getting jealous when they see him manifesting himself in the lives of others. As a result, sometimes you might find your blessing is in the same house, on the same job, and even in the same church as your enemy. I did.

My former pastor walked away with my ex-wife, but I possess the blessing. With no doubt, he obviously and desperately wanted what I had, namely my ex-wife. Most people never knew how I felt about my pastor having an affair with my recently

Legacy of Leadership/Chapter 9

divorced wife, and most people never will. Although, when newspapers made their adulterous affair public, following the tragedy effecting their newborn, again, rumors spread throughout northwest Indiana quickly. Many people speculated and others questioned my perspective. I maintained the same perspective throughout the attacks, accusations, and the entire painful situation. I forgave.

Just as David had already been anointed King, I knew God had already anointed me pastor of New Hope. David continued forgiving Saul and offering sacrifices of praise with his harp. Hence, I followed in his footsteps, I continued forgiving my pastor and singing praises unto God with the choir. Saul ruled in the palace, and my pastor had recently completed construction on our new $2 million facility. David said, "Thou prepares a table before me in the presence of my enemies." Likewise, God had a new facility built so that I could consecrate it unto him as a house of worship. Now that I am senior pastor of New Hope, I am confident that God has a plan for each of our lives. Whatever you're going through, its only preparing you to walk in purpose. Remember, don't allow trials to make you abandon the promise, your enemy and blessing are

I Am Born To Preach The Gospel

oftentimes found in the same place.

Another person the Bible uses to illustrate suffering in the Old Testament book of Genesis 37, is Joseph. Two distinct things about Joseph made others jealous; his ability to interpret dreams, and his father's love. Jacob is Joseph's father, and God changed Jacob's name to Israel. Jacob is his birth name, and Israel represents God's favor. The Bible says "Israel loved Joseph more than his brothers." In other words, God's favor was upon Joseph more than his siblings.

As a result, his brothers hated him so that they could not speak peaceably to him. Jealousy caused them to sell Joseph into slavery. Joseph's biography is quite extensive. Ultimately, by interpreting the Egyptian Pharaoh's dream, he gained great favor. He became governor, ruling throughout the land of Egypt. His interpretation devised a plan to save Egypt during the famine.

Afterward, other nations added to the wealth of Egypt, because they had no where else to buy food. Included in the arrival of those seeking food were Joseph's brothers. His great success left them frozen stiff in panic, but Joseph greeted them in love. He understood that if they hadn't persecuted him, he would not have attained greatness and fulfilled his destiny. Joseph responded to his frightened brothers by forgiving them. As opposed to being angry with his brothers, Joseph explained that everything happens for a reason. Perhaps you're reading this book while facing difficult challenges, don't ever forget that you were born for such a time as this!

Christians must begin believing and speaking that *all things work together for the good to them that love God, and who are called according to his purpose.* When we fully understand what God means by this scripture, "He said, she said," mess, and the negative actions of others will not sway our attitudes. Bad things only happen to good people in order to align us with our destiny. The devil is our enemy, but people are never our problem.

Perhaps men have elevated you, or your ego, into a position of authority. Please understand that God will not anoint you, or give you supernatural power, to lead until you make the decision to live a lifestyle of forgiveness. If you ever plan to experience God's anointing, then you must make a

I Am Born To Preach The Gospel

decision to forgive, even before the opportunity arises.

As I grew older, I discovered that a prominent and well-respected Gary Baptist pastor, Dr. Cato Brooks is my biological uncle. His son, Pastor Terry Brooks is logically my cousin. To my surprise, I learned that my biological father Jerry Akins is an out-of-town pastor. His son, my brother, whom I never met, is Minister Elijah Akins, I'm told he lives in Indianapolis. Between my father's blood lineage, and my mother's father, Pastor Clarence Lobdell, I am the seed of a legacy of leadership. For a certainty, I was born to preach the gospel. Nothing can stop God's promises from manifesting in our lives, especially when we submit to his plan and power.

Today is the first day of the rest of my life, and I plan to carry on this legacy of leadership by preaching God's word in power. I've literally transitioned from the pit to the palace, from defeat to victory, and from sorrow to joy. This is my story, but it doesn't end here My life is a living epistle, read and heard of men. I've suffered these experiences written within this book so that God's glory can be manifested in the lives of every reader!